Contents

Written by
Julia Golding

Illustrated by
Sonia Possentini

Series editor **Dee Reid**

T0352004

PEARSON

Before reading *Wings*

Characters

Gideon

Crystal

Kelsie

New vocabulary

ch1 p7 paramedics
ch2 p8 disguised
ch2 p11 sensed
ch2 p11 wondered

ch3 p16 murmured
ch3 p16 shrugged
ch4 p18 glanced

Introduction

Gideon is a dark angel. He was kicked out of heaven for breaking the rules and he was sent down to earth. He has been on earth for years doing good and helping humans. Now his time on earth is up and the angels are looking for him so that they can take him back to heaven.

Wings

Chapter One

My name is Gideon. I am a dark angel. I was kicked out of heaven for breaking the rules. I didn't help a man make the right decision at a turning point in his life and he ended up dead.

So I've been on earth for years doing good to make up for that mistake. Now I have done enough good and the angels are looking for me to take me home to heaven.

The truth is, I'm not ready to go back. I love this world too much. I like humans, even if they do stupid things sometimes. On earth I'm helping to change people's lives.

An angel friend of mine called Crystal came to see me a few days ago and told me that the Judge had sent her to bring me back to heaven. I begged her to go back on her own and, because she is my friend, she did.

I knew I had to keep my head down and stay out of trouble so that the other angels would not find me. But when I saw a toddler run out in front of a car that was travelling too fast, I couldn't just stand back and watch her die. I ran into the road, grabbed the little girl and pushed her out of the way of the car. The car struck me. I rolled over the car, flew into the air and landed with a terrible thump on the cold, hard ground.

I had been in pain before. I had been shot and stabbed trying to protect humans. Angels are strong but the car had hit me hard. I wasn't able to get up and disappear before the paramedics arrived to take me to hospital.

Chapter Two

The first person I saw coming through the door of my hospital room was an angel. She was disguised as a nurse but I knew straight away that she was an angel messenger. She delivered the news that my time on earth was nearly over. When I had my strength back she would return and take me to face the Judge. Then she left.

My doctor, Kelsie, appeared in the
doorway. She was very beautiful
with dark skin, long hair and
big kind eyes. I remembered that I had helped
her sister, Taylor, many years before. How strange
that I should meet Taylor's sister when my own life
on earth had reached a turning point.

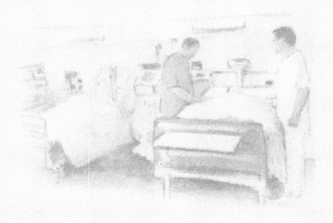

"I've just heard from the toddler's mum," said Kelsie. "The little girl you saved is OK. You were very brave."

I smiled. It was good to go out on a high. I felt my strength returning and I knew the angel messenger would be back for me soon. Kelsie looked worried as I started to climb out of the hospital bed, desperate to get away. "Don't you dare get up," she warned me. "You have just been hit by a car."

She thought she knew what was good for me but each second I stayed here was eating into the time I had to vanish and hide again. I sensed that my time on earth was almost up.

Kelsie felt for my pulse and she shook her head. *Why can't I feel your heart beating?* she wondered.

Then I saw her remembering.

"You're like the guy who saved my sister – the doctors couldn't find his pulse and Taylor said he had some strange scars on his back like yours."

I kept quiet. Kelsie stared at me. Then she said, "It is you, isn't it? Who are you?"

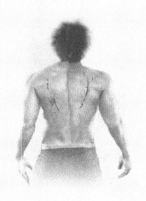

Chapter Three

Suddenly, the angel messenger appeared in the room. I should have gone while I had the chance.

"He's an angel," she said in a low voice.

Kelsie laughed out loud.

"He might have done something very brave but I'm afraid that doesn't make him an angel!"

That was when I fell in love with Kelsie.

The angel could sense that I loved Kelsie. She smiled, then she turned to Kelsie and said, "If you want to help Gideon, come with us now," and the angel spread her wings around us.

For a minute it went dark and then Kelsie and I were standing in a pool of bright light. We were in the centre of a huge crowd of angels. The Judge flew in and everyone went silent.

"Please tell me what is going on," whispered Kelsie. Her whole body was shaking with fear and I felt bad that I had dragged her into this.

"I am to be tried," I told her. "I should have returned to heaven but I made the choice to stay on earth. I've broken the rules of heaven."

"What will happen to you?" murmured Kelsie.

I shrugged.

She touched my arm. "I won't let them hurt you."

The Judge held up his hand for silence.

Chapter Four

"Gideon, your time is up," said the Judge. "You cannot stay on earth as a fallen angel any longer. You must make up your mind: you can live with the fallen angels in darkness, or you can return to heaven and have your wings back."

It would be torture living in darkness with the

fallen angels because I would still have my powers

but I would never be able to help anyone. But if I

returned to heaven I would not be able to spend

time with Kelsie. I wanted my wings back but, as I

glanced at Kelsie, I realised what I wanted more.

I fixed my eyes on the Judge.

"I want to be human," I said. The angels cried out

in horror.

"Do you know what that means?" gasped

the Judge. "If I make you human, one day you

will die."

"Yes. But I want to live in this world first,"
I explained. I saw Kelsie move towards me, her
eyes shining with tears.

"You are the first angel to ask to be made
human," the Judge said. "I will give you your
wish because you love this world more than
you love heaven."

The angels began to leave, still looking shocked. Crystal, my old friend, stayed behind for a moment. "I wish you a good life, Gideon," she said. "Maybe I'll see you on the other side when your human life is over." Then she flew off.

I couldn't believe it – I felt so alive! A tattoo of wings appeared on my back in place of my old scars.

"Did that really all just happen?" asked Kelsie.

"Yes," I said. "They set me free to be human."

"What are you going to do now?" asked Kelsie.

"Live," I replied.

"By yourself?" she asked.

I gave her my hand. "Not if there's someone who will put up with me."

Kelsie took my hand. "I think there's a very good chance of that," she said.

As the sun rose, we walked off to start our new life.

Quiz

p4 Why are the angels looking for Gideon?
a) He is lost.
b) To take him home to heaven.
c) They haven't seen him for a long time.

p4 Why does Gideon want to stay on earth?
a) He loved heaven too much.
b) He likes being a fallen angel.
c) He wanted to help change people's lives.

p14 Why did the angel messenger want Kelsie to go with Gideon?
a) She thought Kelsie could help Gideon.
b) She wanted to show Kelsie some other angels.
c) She knew Gideon was an angel.

p18 What does it mean for Gideon if he chooses to be human?
a) He will get his wings back.
b) He will still have angel powers.
c) He will die one day.

p19 Why did the Judge grant Gideon his wish?
a) He knew Gideon loved heaven more than earth.
b) He knew Gideon loved earth more than heaven.
c) He wanted Gideon to live with the fallen angels.

Inferential comprehension

- Why did Gideon want to disappear after the accident?

- What strange things does Kelsie notice about Gideon?

- Why did the angels cry out in horror?

- What evidence is there that the angel Judge is fair?

- What evidence is there that Gideon has done good on earth?

rsonal response

- Do you think it is fair that Gideon was thrown out of heaven?

- Would you have gone with the angel messenger and Gideon?

- Would you have chosen to stay on earth?

- What would be the best thing about being an angel?

Published by Pearson Education Limited, Edinburgh Gate, Harlow, Essex, CM20 2JE.

www.pearsonschoolsandfecolleges.co.uk

Text © Pearson Education Limited 2012

Edited by Jo Dilloway
Designed by Siu Hang Wong
Original illustrations © Pearson Education Limited 2012
Illustrated by Sonia Possentini
Cover design by Siu Hang Wong
Cover illustration © Pearson Education Limited 2012

The right of Julia Golding to be identified as author of this work has been asserted by her in
accordance with the Copyright, Designs and Patents Act 1988.

First published 2012

2023
15

British Library Cataloguing in Publication Data
A catalogue record for this book is available from the British Library

ISBN 978 0 435 07165 3

Printed in Great Britain by Ashford Colour Press Ltd.